The Crypto Millionaire Handbook: How to Easily Make Life-Changing Money in The Next Big 2024-2025 Bull Run with Smart Investing and Trading Any Cryptocurrency (Altcoins, Meme, NFT, Airdrops): With questions that will help you know more about crypto.

PRESTINE JERRY

All rights reserved.

This work may not be reproduced, distributed, or transmitted in any form or by any means, including photocopying, recording, or other electronic or mechanical methods, without the prior written permission of the writer, except in the case of brief quotations embodied in critical reviews and certain other noncommercial uses permitted by copyright law.

TABLE OF CONTENT

Chapter 1: Introduction to Cryptocurrency

- Understanding the Basics: What is Cryptocurrency?
- History and Evolution of Digital Currencies
- Key Terminology and Concepts
- The Importance of Blockchain Technology
- The Rise of Bitcoin and Beyond: Altcoins

Chapter 2: The 2024-2025 Bull Run: What to Expect

- Historical Bull Runs: Lessons from the Past
- Indicators of a Bull Market
- Predicting the 2024-2025 Bull Run: Factors to Consider
- Preparing for Market Volatility
- Setting Realistic Expectations and Goals

Chapter 3: Identifying Promising Altcoins

- What Are Altcoins?
- Criteria for Evaluating Altcoins
- Top Altcoins to Watch in 2024-2025
- Case Studies: Successful Altcoin Investments
- Tools and Resources for Altcoin Analysis

Chapter 4: Meme Coins: High Risk, High Reward

- The Phenomenon of Meme Coins
- Popular Meme Coins and Their Histories
- Analyzing the Potential of Meme Coins
- Risks Associated with Meme Coin Investments
- Strategies for Investing in Meme Coins

Chapter 5: The World of NFTs (Non-Fungible Token*

- Understanding NFTs and Their Value
- The NFT Marketplace: Platforms and Trends
- How to Invest in NFTs
- Success Stories and Cautionary Tales
- Future Outlook for NFTs

Chapter 6: Profiting from Airdrops

- What Are Airdrops and How Do They Work?
- Identifying Valuable Airdrops
- Steps to Participate in Airdrops
- Risks and Considerations
- Maximizing Profits from Airdrops

Chapter 7: Smart Investing Strategies

- Diversification: Spreading Your Investments
- Fundamental and Technical Analysis
- Long-Term vs. Short-Term Investments
- Portfolio Management Tips
- Avoiding Common Investment Pitfalls

Chapter 8: Securing Your Cryptocurrency Investments

- Understanding the Risks
- Wallet Management
- Best Practices for Wallet Security
- Safeguarding Private Keys
- Recognizing and Avoiding Scams
- Ensuring Overall Security

-Case Studies: Security Breaches and Lessons Learned
-Future Trends in Cryptocurrency Security

Chapter 9: Security and Risk Management

- Protecting Your Investments: Wallets and Exchanges
- Recognizing and Avoiding Scams
- Regulatory Considerations
- Managing Emotional and Psychological Risks
- Insurance and Backup Plans

Chapter 10: Q&A: Deepening Your Crypto Knowledge**

- Essential Questions to Ask Before Investing
- Case Studies and Real-World Scenarios
- Expert Opinions and Insights
- Self-Assessment: Gauging Your Crypto Readiness
- Continuous Learning and Staying Informed

Each chapter in "The Crypto Millionaire Handbook" is designed to equip you with the knowledge and tools necessary to thrive in the dynamic world of cryptocurrency. From understanding the basics to mastering advanced strategies, this book aims to guide you toward financial success in the upcoming bull run.

Introduction to The Crypto Millionaire Handbook

Maria Sanchez, NOT Coin Airdrop Recipient "I couldn't believe my luck when I received the NOT Coin airdrop! I had signed up on a whim, thinking it might be a fun experiment. When the tokens hit my wallet, I was skeptical at first. But as the weeks went by, the value of NOT Coin started to climb rapidly. I decided to hold onto them, and within a few months, my initial airdrop had turned into a substantial amount. It was a life-changing experience that gave me the confidence to dive deeper into the world of cryptocurrency."

Welcome to "The Crypto Millionaire Handbook: How to Easily Make Life-Changing Money in The Next Big 2024-2025 Bull Run with Smart Investing and Trading Any Cryptocurrency (Altcoins, Meme, NFT, Airdrops)." This comprehensive guide is your essential roadmap to navigating the exhilarating and often unpredictable world of cryptocurrency. Whether you're a seasoned investor or a complete novice, this book offers valuable insights and practical strategies designed to help you capitalize on the upcoming 2024-2025 bull run.

In this handbook, you'll discover how to identify and invest in promising altcoins, meme coins, NFTs, and airdrops, enabling you to maximize your returns. The book demystifies complex concepts and provides a clear, actionable framework for smart investing and trading. You'll learn to recognize market trends, manage risks effectively, and make informed decisions that can lead to substantial financial gains.

Additionally, "The Crypto Millionaire Handbook" includes a series of thought-provoking questions that will deepen your understanding of the crypto market and help you formulate a personalized investment strategy.

These questions are designed to guide your learning and ensure that you are well-prepared to seize the opportunities presented by the next big bull run.

Prepare to embark on a journey that could transform your financial future. With the right knowledge and approach, achieving millionaire status through cryptocurrency investing is within your reach. This book is your ultimate guide to making life-changing money in the exciting world of digital assets.

Chapter 1: Introduction to Cryptocurrency

Cryptocurrency has emerged as one of the most revolutionary innovations in the financial world. It represents a paradigm shift from traditional fiat currencies and banking systems to a decentralized and digital form of money. Understanding cryptocurrency is crucial for anyone looking to navigate and profit from this dynamic and rapidly evolving market.

Understanding the Basics: What is Cryptocurrency?

At its core, cryptocurrency is a form of digital or virtual currency that uses cryptography for security. Unlike traditional currencies issued by governments and central banks, cryptocurrencies operate on decentralized networks based on blockchain technology. This decentralization makes them immune to government interference and manipulation, providing a level of security and transparency previously unattainable in the financial sector.

History and Evolution of Digital Currencies

The concept of digital currency is not entirely new. However, the creation of Bitcoin in 2009 by an anonymous entity known as Satoshi Nakamoto marked the birth of modern cryptocurrencies. Bitcoin was designed as a peer-to-peer electronic cash system, allowing users to send and receive payments without the need for intermediaries like banks.

Since the introduction of Bitcoin, thousands of alternative cryptocurrencies, or altcoins, have been developed, each with its unique features and use cases.

These range from Ethereum, which introduced smart contracts, to newer innovations like meme coins and NFTs (Non-Fungible Tokens).

Key Terminology and Concepts

To navigate the world of cryptocurrency, it's essential to familiarize yourself with some key terms:

Blockchain: A decentralized ledger of all transactions across a network. This technology underpins cryptocurrencies and ensures transparency and security.

- Mining: The process of validating and adding new transactions to the blockchain, typically in exchange for a reward in the form of cryptocurrency.
-
Wallet: A digital tool that allows you to store, send, and receive cryptocurrencies. Wallets can be hardware-based (physical devices) or software-based (online or mobile apps).

-Exchange: A platform where you can buy, sell, and trade cryptocurrencies.

- Decentralization: The principle of distributing power and decision-making away from a central authority.

The Importance of Blockchain Technology

Blockchain technology is the backbone of cryptocurrencies. It is a distributed ledger that records all transactions across a network of computers. This structure ensures that no single entity has control over the entire network, enhancing security and transparency.

Each block in the blockchain contains a list of transactions and is linked to the previous block, forming a chain. This immutability makes blockchain highly resistant to fraud and hacking.

The Rise of Bitcoin and Beyond: Altcoins

Bitcoin is often referred to as digital gold due to its finite supply and store of value properties. However, the cryptocurrency market has expanded far beyond Bitcoin.
Altcoins, or alternative cryptocurrencies, have been developed to address various limitations of Bitcoin and introduce new functionalities.

- Ethereum: Known for its smart contract functionality, Ethereum allows developers to build decentralized applications (DApps) on its platform.

- Ripple (XRP): Focuses on facilitating cross-border payments and reducing transaction times and costs.

- Litecoin (LTC): Often described as the silver to Bitcoin's gold, it offers faster transaction confirmation times.

As the cryptocurrency landscape continues to evolve, new projects and technologies emerge, offering diverse investment opportunities.

The Future of Cryptocurrency

Cryptocurrencies are still in their early stages of development and adoption.

As technology advances and more people recognize the benefits of decentralized finance, the role of cryptocurrencies in the global economy is expected to grow. Regulatory frameworks are also evolving, which will provide more clarity and potentially increase mainstream adoption.

In the following chapters, we will delve deeper into the various aspects of cryptocurrency investing and trading. You'll learn how to identify promising investment opportunities, manage risks, and develop strategies to make life-changing money in the upcoming 2024-2025 bull run. Prepare yourself for an exciting journey into the world of digital assets.

Chapter 2: The 2024-2025 Bull Run: What to Expect

As the cryptocurrency market matures, it continues to experience cycles of rapid growth followed by corrections. These cycles, known as bull and bear markets, are driven by a combination of technological advancements, regulatory developments, market sentiment, and macroeconomic factors. Understanding the dynamics of these cycles is crucial for making informed investment decisions and maximizing your returns during the next big bull run.

Historical Bull Runs: Lessons from the Past

To anticipate and prepare for the 2024-2025 bull run, it's essential to examine previous bull markets. Historical bull runs have been characterized by significant price increases, widespread media attention, and a surge in new investors entering the market. Key takeaways from past bull runs include:

- 2013 Bull Run: Bitcoin's price surged from around $100 to over $1,000. This period saw the initial mainstream awareness of cryptocurrency, driven by media coverage and increased adoption.

-2017 Bull Run: Bitcoin reached nearly $20,000, and Ethereum saw substantial gains. The ICO (Initial Coin Offering) boom fueled speculative investments, leading to an influx of new projects and investors.

- 2020-2021 Bull Run: Bitcoin hit an all-time high of over $60,000, with significant gains in altcoins and the rise of DeFi (Decentralized Finance) and NFTs. Institutional adoption and macroeconomic factors, such as stimulus measures, played a crucial role.

By studying these patterns, we can identify common factors that may signal the onset of the next bull run.

Indicators of a Bull Market

Several indicators can help predict the start of a bull market. While no single factor guarantees a bull run, a combination of these signals increases the likelihood:

- Increased Institutional Investment: When major financial institutions and corporations begin investing in cryptocurrencies, it signals confidence in the market's future potential.

- Regulatory Clarity: Clear and favorable regulatory developments can reduce uncertainty and attract more investors.

- Technological Advancements: Innovations in blockchain technology, such as scalability solutions and new use cases, can drive interest and adoption.

- Market Sentiment: Positive news coverage, social media buzz, and influential endorsements can create a bullish sentiment.

- Macroeconomic Factors: Economic conditions, such as inflation or monetary policy changes, can impact investor behavior and drive interest in alternative assets like cryptocurrencies.

Predicting the 2024-2025 Bull Run: Factors to Consider

The upcoming bull run will likely be influenced by several key factors:

- Mainstream Adoption: Continued growth in the adoption of cryptocurrencies by businesses and consumers will drive demand.

- Regulatory Environment**: Developments in crypto regulation, both positive and negative, will shape market dynamics.

-Technological Breakthroughs**: Innovations such as Ethereum 2.0, Layer 2 solutions, and cross-chain interoperability could attract new users and investors.

-Global Economic Conditions**: Economic instability or favorable conditions for alternative assets could push more investors toward cryptocurrencies.

Preparing for Market Volatility

While bull markets offer significant profit potential, they also come with increased volatility. Prices can swing dramatically, driven by speculation and market sentiment. To navigate this volatility, consider the following strategies:

-Diversification: Spread your investments across multiple cryptocurrencies to mitigate risk.

-Risk Management: Set stop-loss orders and take-profit levels to protect your gains and limit losses.

- Stay Informed: Keep up with market news, regulatory updates, and technological developments to make informed decisions.

-Emotional Discipline: Avoid making impulsive decisions based on market hype or fear. Stick to your investment plan.

Setting Realistic Expectations and Goals

It's important to approach the 2024-2025 bull run with realistic expectations. While it's possible to achieve significant returns, it's also essential to recognize the inherent risks
 Set clear investment goals, whether it's long-term wealth accumulation or short-term gains, and develop a strategy aligned with your risk tolerance and financial objectives.

In the next chapters, we will delve into specific investment opportunities within the cryptocurrency market, including altcoins, meme coins, NFTs, and airdrops. By understanding these areas, you'll be better equipped to capitalize on the opportunities presented by the upcoming bull run.

Chapter 3: Identifying Promising Altcoins

As the cryptocurrency market continues to expand, altcoins offer significant opportunities for investors seeking to diversify their portfolios beyond Bitcoin. Altcoins, or alternative cryptocurrencies, are developed to address various limitations of Bitcoin or to introduce new functionalities and use cases. In this chapter, we will explore how to identify promising altcoins, evaluate their potential, and make informed investment decisions.

What Are Altcoins?

Altcoins encompass all cryptocurrencies other than Bitcoin. They can range from well-established projects like Ethereum to newly launched tokens with specific use cases. Altcoins often aim to improve upon Bitcoin's technology, offering enhanced features such as faster transaction times, lower fees, or additional functionality through smart contracts and decentralized applications (DApps).

Criteria for Evaluating Altcoins

When evaluating altcoins, consider the following criteria to determine their potential:

- Technology and Innovation: Assess the technological advancements and innovations that the altcoin brings to the table. Does it solve a real problem or improve upon existing solutions?

- Team and Development: Research the team behind the altcoin. Experienced and reputable developers and advisors can significantly impact a project's success.

- Use Case and Adoption: Determine the altcoin's use case and its potential for widespread adoption. Is there a real demand for the solution it offers?

-Market Capitalization and Volume: Analyze the altcoin's market capitalization and trading volume. Higher market cap and volume can indicate greater stability and investor interest.

-Community and Support: A strong and active community can drive the success of an altcoin. Look for active social media presence, forums, and developer engagement.

-Partnerships and Collaborations: Strategic partnerships and collaborations can enhance an altcoin's credibility and potential for growth.

Top Altcoins to Watch in 2024-2025

While the cryptocurrency market is highly dynamic, certain altcoins have shown consistent promise and potential for growth. Here are a few to watch in the upcoming bull run:

-Ethereum (ETH): As the second-largest cryptocurrency by market cap, Ethereum is a foundational platform for smart contracts and DApps. The transition to Ethereum 2.0 aims to improve scalability and reduce energy consumption.

-Cardano (ADA): Known for its research-driven approach and strong emphasis on security and scalability, Cardano aims to create a more balanced and sustainable ecosystem for cryptocurrencies.

Polkadot (DOT): Polkadot focuses on interoperability between different blockchains, enabling them to communicate and share information securely and efficiently.

-Solana (SOL): With its high throughput and low transaction costs, Solana is gaining popularity for its ability to support decentralized applications and DeFi projects.

-Chainlink (LINK): As a decentralized oracle network, Chainlink provides reliable and secure connections between smart contracts and real-world data.

Case Studies: Successful Altcoin Investments

Examining successful altcoin investments can provide valuable insights into what factors contribute to their growth. Here are a few examples:

-Binance Coin (BNB): Initially launched as a utility token for the Binance exchange, BNB has grown significantly, offering various use cases within the Binance ecosystem, including transaction fee discounts and participation in token sales.

-Uniswap (UNI): As a leading decentralized exchange (DEX), Uniswap has revolutionized the way users trade cryptocurrencies by enabling trustless and permissionless trading directly from their wallets.

- Avalanche (AVAX): Avalanche has gained attention for its high throughput, low latency, and compatibility with Ethereum, attracting developers and projects seeking scalability.

Tools and Resources for Altcoin Analysis

To effectively analyze and track altcoins, utilize the following tools and resources:

- CoinMarketCap and CoinGecko: These platforms provide comprehensive data on cryptocurrencies, including price charts, market cap, trading volume, and historical data.

- Whitepapers and Official Websites: Review the altcoin's whitepaper and official website to understand its technology, use case, and roadmap.

- Social Media and Community Forums: Engage with the altcoin's community on platforms like Twitter, Reddit, and Telegram to gauge sentiment and stay updated on developments.

- Technical Analysis Tools: Use charting tools like TradingView to perform technical analysis and identify potential entry and exit points.

- News Outlets and Blogs: Follow reputable cryptocurrency news outlets and blogs to stay informed about market trends, regulatory changes, and significant developments.

By applying these criteria and utilizing these tools, you can identify promising altcoins with the potential for significant returns.

In the next chapters, we will explore other lucrative areas of the cryptocurrency market, including meme coins, NFTs, and airdrops, providing you with a comprehensive understanding of various investment opportunities.

Chapter 4: Meme Coins: High Risk, High Reward

Meme coins have gained immense popularity in the cryptocurrency market due to their viral nature and the communities that rally behind them. Unlike traditional cryptocurrencies, meme coins are often inspired by internet memes or jokes, and their value can be driven more by social media trends and community engagement than by underlying technology or use cases. In this chapter, we will explore the world of meme coins, analyze their potential risks and rewards, and provide strategies for investing in these volatile assets.

The Phenomenon of Meme Coins

Meme coins are a unique subset of cryptocurrencies that have captured the attention of both investors and the general public. The most notable examples include Dogecoin (DOGE) and Shiba Inu (SHIB), both of which started as jokes but grew to become major players in the market. The success of these coins can be attributed to their strong communities, social media influence, and celebrity endorsements.

-Dogecoin (DOGE): Created in 2013 as a parody of Bitcoin, Dogecoin features the Shiba Inu dog from the "Doge" meme. Despite its origins as a joke, Dogecoin has seen significant price increases, partly due to endorsements from celebrities like Elon Musk.

-Shiba Inu (SHIB): Dubbed the "Dogecoin killer," Shiba Inu capitalized on the popularity of Dogecoin and the meme culture surrounding it. SHIB has developed its ecosystem, including ShibaSwap, a decentralized exchange.

Popular Meme Coins and Their Histories

To better understand meme coins, it's helpful to look at their backgrounds and how they achieved popularity:

-SafeMoon (SAFEMOON): Launched in March 2021, SafeMoon introduced a unique tokenomics model that rewards holders and penalizes sellers with transaction fees, which are redistributed to existing holders.

-Akita Inu (AKITA): Similar to Shiba Inu, Akita Inu is another meme coin that gained traction through social media and community support. It aims to create a decentralized ecosystem with various use cases.

-Floki Inu (FLOKI): Named after Elon Musk's dog, Floki Inu leverages the meme coin trend and aims to create a full ecosystem, including an NFT marketplace and educational platform.

Analyzing the Potential of Meme Coins

Investing in meme coins can be lucrative, but it requires careful analysis and an understanding of their unique dynamics:

- Community and Social Media Presence: The strength and activity of the community are crucial for a meme coin's success. A vibrant community can drive demand and sustain interest.

- Celebrity Endorsements and Influences: Public endorsements from influential figures can lead to significant price increases. However, reliance on such endorsements can also lead to volatility.

- Market Sentiment and Trends: Meme coins are highly sensitive to market sentiment and trends. Staying updated on social media trends and market sentiment is essential for timing investments.

-Tokenomics and Utility: While many meme coins start as jokes, some develop unique tokenomics and utility over time. Evaluating the token's economics and potential use cases can provide insights into its long-term viability.

Risks Associated with Meme Coin Investments

Meme coins come with high risks, and it's important to be aware of the potential pitfalls:

-Volatility**: Meme coins are extremely volatile, with prices subject to rapid and significant fluctuations. This volatility can lead to substantial gains or losses in a short period.

-Lack of Fundamental Value: Many meme coins lack intrinsic value or a clear use case, making their prices heavily dependent on market sentiment and hype.

-Scams and Rug Pulls: The meme coin market is rife with scams and projects designed to pump and dump. Always conduct thorough research and due diligence before investing.

-Regulatory Uncertainty: As meme coins often operate in a legal gray area, they may face regulatory scrutiny that could impact their value and viability.

Strategies for Investing in Meme Coins

To navigate the high-risk, high-reward nature of meme coins, consider the following strategies:

-Diversification: Spread your investments across multiple meme coins and other types of cryptocurrencies to mitigate risk.

-Research and Due Diligence: Thoroughly research each meme coin, including its community, developers, and market sentiment. Look for transparency and active development.

-Set Clear Entry and Exit Points: Define your investment goals and set clear entry and exit points to manage your risk and lock in profits.

-Stay Updated on Trends: Monitor social media platforms, forums, and news outlets to stay informed about trends and sentiment shifts in the meme coin market.

-Use Risk Management Techniques: Implement risk management techniques such as stop-loss orders and position sizing to protect your investments.

In conclusion, meme coins offer the potential for significant rewards, but they also come with considerable risks. By understanding the unique dynamics of meme coins, conducting thorough research, and employing sound investment strategies, you can navigate this volatile market and potentially capitalize on its opportunities. In the next chapter, we will explore the world of NFTs (Non-Fungible Tokens) and their growing influence in the cryptocurrency space.

Chapter 5: The World of NFTs (Non-Fungible Tokens)

Non-Fungible Tokens (NFTs) have become one of the most exciting and talked-about innovations in the cryptocurrency space. Unlike traditional cryptocurrencies, which are fungible and can be exchanged on a one-to-one basis, NFTs are unique digital assets that represent ownership of a specific item or piece of content. This chapter will explore what NFTs are, their value propositions, the current marketplace, how to invest in them, and the future outlook for NFTs.

Understanding NFTs and Their Value

NFTs are digital tokens that use blockchain technology to certify the ownership and authenticity of a unique asset. These assets can include digital art, music, virtual real estate, collectibles, and more. The uniqueness and indivisibility of NFTs distinguish them from cryptocurrencies like Bitcoin or Ethereum, which are interchangeable.

Key Features of NFTs:
- Uniqueness: Each NFT has distinct information that makes it different from any other token.
- Indivisibility: NFTs cannot be divided into smaller units; they exist as whole items.
- Ownership and Provenance: NFTs provide a clear chain of ownership and provenance, ensuring that the asset's history and authenticity can be verified.

The NFT Marketplace: Platforms and Trends

The NFT marketplace has seen explosive growth, with several platforms emerging as leaders in the space. Some of the most popular NFT marketplaces include:

- OpenSea: One of the largest and most diverse NFT marketplaces, OpenSea offers a wide range of digital assets, from art and collectibles to virtual real estate.

- Rarible: A decentralized marketplace where users can create, buy, and sell NFTs. Rarible also has its governance token, RARI, which allows holders to participate in platform decisions.

- Foundation: A platform focused on digital art, Foundation provides a space for artists to mint and auction their work as NFTs.

- SuperRare: An exclusive marketplace for digital art, SuperRare emphasizes high-quality, curated works and a strong artist community.

- Decentraland: A virtual world where users can buy, sell, and trade virtual real estate and other digital assets using NFTs.

Current Trends in the NFT Market:

- Digital Art: NFTs have revolutionized the art world by enabling artists to monetize their digital creations directly. High-profile sales, such as Beeple's "Everydays: The First 5000 Days," which sold for $69 million, have garnered significant attention.

- Gaming: NFTs are being integrated into the gaming industry, allowing players to own and trade in-game assets. Games like Axie Infinity and The Sandbox have pioneered this model.

- **Virtual Real Estate:** Platforms like Decentraland and Cryptovoxels allow users to purchase, develop, and trade virtual land and properties.

- **Collectibles:** NFT collectibles, such as CryptoPunks and Bored Ape Yacht Club, have created vibrant communities and markets around rare and unique items.

How to Invest in NFTs?

Investing in NFTs requires a different approach compared to traditional cryptocurrencies. Here are some steps and considerations to help you get started:

- **Choose a Marketplace:** Select an NFT marketplace that aligns with your interests, whether it's digital art, gaming, or virtual real estate.

- **Set Up a Wallet:** To purchase NFTs, you need a digital wallet that supports the blockchain the NFTs are built on, typically Ethereum. Examples include MetaMask and Trust Wallet.

- **Fund Your Wallet:** Transfer cryptocurrency, usually Ether (ETH), to your wallet to use for purchasing NFTs.

- **Research and Due Diligence:** Investigate the NFT project, the creators, and the community. Look for indicators of value, such as the artist's reputation, the rarity of the item, and the demand within the community.

- **Purchase and Secure Your NFT:** Once you find an NFT you want to invest in, complete the purchase through the marketplace. Ensure your NFT is stored securely in your digital wallet.

Success Stories and Cautionary Tales

The NFT market has produced numerous success stories, but it also comes with risks. Understanding both sides can help you make informed decisions:

Success Stories:

- **Beeple's Digital Art:** The sale of Beeple's digital artwork for $69 million at Christie's auction house brought mainstream attention to NFTs and highlighted their potential value.

- **CryptoPunks:** These 10,000 unique, algorithmically generated characters were some of the first NFTs on the Ethereum blockchain and have since become highly valuable collectibles.

Cautionary Tales:

- **Market Volatility:** The value of NFTs can be highly volatile, with prices subject to significant fluctuations based on market sentiment and trends.

- **Scams and Fraud:** As with any emerging market, the NFT space has seen its share of scams. Ensure you are buying from reputable sources and verify the authenticity of the NFT.

- **Environmental Concerns:** The energy consumption associated with minting and transacting NFTs on certain blockchains has raised environmental concerns, leading to calls for more sustainable practices.

Future Outlook for NFTs

The future of NFTs looks promising, with potential applications extending beyond the current trends. Key areas to watch include:

- **Integration with the Metaverse:** As virtual worlds and the metaverse concept evolve, NFTs will likely play a crucial role in digital ownership and commerce.

- **Expansion into Traditional Industries:** Industries such as real estate, entertainment, and fashion are exploring the use of NFTs for tokenizing physical assets and enhancing customer engagement.

- **Technological Advancements:** Improvements in blockchain technology, such as Ethereum 2.0 and Layer 2 solutions, will address scalability and environmental concerns, making NFTs more accessible and sustainable.

In conclusion, NFTs represent a significant and rapidly growing segment of the cryptocurrency market, offering unique opportunities for investors and creators alike. By understanding their value, navigating the marketplace, and staying informed about trends and risks, you can capitalize on the potential of NFTs. In the next chapter, we will explore the lucrative world of airdrops and how to profit from these free distributions of cryptocurrency tokens.

Chapter 6: Profiting from Airdrops

Airdrops are a unique and exciting aspect of the cryptocurrency market. They involve the distribution of free tokens to a large number of wallet addresses, usually to promote a new cryptocurrency project or reward loyal users. For investors, airdrops present an opportunity to acquire new tokens without an initial investment. This chapter will explain what airdrops are, how they work, and how you can identify and profit from them.

Understanding Airdrops

Airdrops are a marketing strategy used by cryptocurrency projects to generate interest, reward loyal community members, and distribute tokens widely. The basic premise is simple: tokens are distributed for free to eligible participants. There are several types of airdrops, each with different criteria and distribution methods.

Types of Airdrops:

- **Standard Airdrops:** Tokens are distributed to existing holders of a specific cryptocurrency, usually based on a snapshot of their wallet balances.

- **Bounty Airdrops:** Participants receive tokens in exchange for completing specific tasks, such as promoting the project on social media, joining a Telegram group, or subscribing to a newsletter.

- **Exclusive Airdrops:** Distributed to select individuals, often early supporters, influential community members, or winners of competitions and giveaways.

- **Holder Airdrops:** Distributed to users who hold a specific cryptocurrency in their wallets at the time of the snapshot.

How Airdrops Work

To participate in an airdrop, you generally need to meet certain eligibility criteria set by the project. These criteria can vary widely depending on the type of airdrop. Here's how you can typically get involved:

1. **Create a Compatible Wallet:** Ensure you have a cryptocurrency wallet compatible with the blockchain on which the airdrop will be distributed (e.g., Ethereum, Binance Smart Chain).
2. **Meet Eligibility Requirements:** Fulfill any specific criteria required by the airdrop, such as holding a particular cryptocurrency, joining social media channels, or performing promotional tasks.
3. **Register for the Airdrop:** Some airdrops require you to register your wallet address on the project's website or through a form.
4. **Receive Tokens:** If you meet the criteria, the airdropped tokens will be sent directly to your wallet. This can happen automatically or after the airdrop campaign ends.

Identifying Promising Airdrops

Not all airdrops are worth pursuing. Here are some factors to consider when evaluating the potential of an airdrop:

- **Project Credibility:** Research the team behind the project, their track record, and their vision. A reputable project with a clear roadmap is more likely to succeed.
- **Community Engagement:** Active and engaged communities often indicate a strong support base and potential for growth.
- **Token Utility:** Assess the token's use case and its role within the project's ecosystem. Tokens with real utility are more likely to hold value.

- **Partnerships and Backers:** Projects backed by reputable investors or partnered with established companies are generally more credible.

- **Market Demand:** Analyze the market demand for the project's solution. A project addressing a real problem with a viable solution is more likely to gain traction.

Strategies for Profiting from Airdrops
To maximize your profits from airdrops, consider the following strategies:

- **Stay Informed:** Join cryptocurrency forums, follow airdrop-focused social media accounts, and subscribe to newsletters that announce upcoming airdrops.

- **Diversify Participation:** Participate in multiple airdrops to increase your chances of receiving valuable tokens. However, prioritize quality over quantity to avoid scams and low-value tokens.

- **Secure Your Wallet:** Use a secure, private wallet to receive airdrops. Avoid sharing your private keys or sensitive information.

- **Sell or Hold?:** Decide whether to sell the airdropped tokens immediately or hold them for potential future gains. This decision should be based on your research and market conditions.

- **Engage with the Community:** Actively participate in the project's community to stay updated on developments and future opportunities. Engaging with the community can also increase your chances of being eligible for exclusive airdrops.

Case Studies: Successful Airdrops

- Examining successful airdrops can provide valuable insights into what factors contribute to their success:

- **Uniswap (UNI) Airdrop:** In September 2020, Uniswap distributed 400 UNI tokens to users who had interacted with the protocol before a specific date. At its peak, the airdrop was worth thousands of dollars per user, highlighting the potential value of participating in early-stage projects.

- **Stellar (XLM) Airdrop:** Stellar conducted multiple airdrops to promote its ecosystem, including a notable one where it distributed 2 billion XLM tokens to verified Keybase users. These airdrops significantly increased awareness and adoption of the Stellar network.

- **OmiseGO (OMG) Airdrop:** In 2017, OmiseGO distributed OMG tokens to Ethereum holders, boosting its user base and market presence. The airdrop recipients benefited from substantial price appreciation as the project gained traction.

Potential Risks and How to Mitigate Them

While airdrops can be lucrative, they also come with risks. Here are some potential risks and ways to mitigate them:

- **Scams and Phishing Attacks:** Be wary of airdrop scams that ask for private keys or other sensitive information. Always verify the legitimacy of the project and use official channels for participation.

Chapter 7: Smart Investing and Trading Strategies

Navigating the cryptocurrency market requires a blend of strategic investing and trading approaches. Unlike traditional markets, the crypto market is characterized by its volatility, rapid developments, and diverse range of assets. This chapter will provide you with smart investing and trading strategies tailored for the unique dynamics of the cryptocurrency space.

Understanding the Basics: Investing vs. Trading
Before diving into specific strategies, it's crucial to distinguish between investing and trading in cryptocurrencies:

- **Investing:** This involves buying and holding cryptocurrencies for an extended period, with the expectation that their value will increase over time. Investors typically focus on long-term growth and may choose assets based on their fundamental value and potential for widespread adoption.

- **Trading:** Trading involves buying and selling cryptocurrencies over shorter time frames to capitalize on market fluctuations. Traders use technical analysis, market trends, and various strategies to make profits from price movements.

Both approaches can be profitable, but they require different mindsets and skill sets.

Long-Term Investing Strategies:

For those who prefer a long-term approach, here are some key strategies to consider:

- **HODLing:** A popular term in the crypto community, HODLing refers to holding onto your cryptocurrencies despite market volatility. This strategy is based on the belief that the long-term potential of cryptocurrencies will outweigh short-term price fluctuations.

- **Dollar-Cost Averaging (DCA):** DCA involves regularly investing a fixed amount of money into a cryptocurrency, regardless of its price. This method helps mitigate the impact of volatility and reduces the risk of making poorly timed investments.

- **Fundamental Analysis:** Evaluate the intrinsic value of a cryptocurrency by analyzing factors such as the team behind it, technology, use case, and market demand. Invest in projects with strong fundamentals and long-term potential.

- **Staking and Yield Farming:** Some cryptocurrencies offer staking or yield farming opportunities, allowing you to earn passive income by locking up your tokens in a network or providing liquidity to a decentralized finance (DeFi) protocol.

Short-Term Trading Strategies

- For those interested in trading, here are some strategies to help you capitalize on short-term market movements:

- **Day Trading:** This strategy involves making multiple trades within a single day, aiming to profit from intraday price movements. Day traders rely heavily on technical analysis, chart patterns, and real-time market data.

- **Swing Trading:** Swing trading involves holding onto a cryptocurrency for several days or weeks to profit from expected upward or downward market swings. This strategy combines technical and fundamental analysis to identify entry and exit points.

- **Scalping:** Scalping is a high-frequency trading strategy that aims to make small profits from numerous trades throughout the day. Scalpers typically use leverage and focus on highly liquid markets.

- **Momentum Trading:** This strategy involves identifying and trading cryptocurrencies that show strong momentum in a particular direction. Momentum traders aim to ride the trend until it shows signs of reversal.

Tools and Resources for Smart Investing and Trading. Leveraging the right tools and resources can enhance your investing and trading success:

- **Technical Analysis Tools:** Platforms like TradingView offer advanced charting tools, indicators, and analysis to help you make informed trading decisions.

- **Fundamental Analysis Resources:** Websites such as CoinMarketCap, CoinGecko, and project whitepapers provide valuable insights into the fundamentals of various cryptocurrencies.

- **News and Updates:** Stay informed about market news, regulatory developments, and project updates through reputable sources like CoinDesk, CoinTelegraph, and crypto-specific social media accounts.

- **Portfolio Trackers:** Use portfolio trackers like Blockfolio or Delta to monitor your investments and track performance in real-time.

Risk Management Techniques

Effective risk management is crucial in the volatile world of cryptocurrencies. Here are some techniques to protect your investments:

- **Diversification:** Spread your investments across different cryptocurrencies and asset classes to reduce risk. Diversification can help mitigate the impact of poor performance in a single asset.
- **Stop-Loss Orders:** Set stop-loss orders to automatically sell a cryptocurrency when its price falls to a predetermined level. This can help limit your losses and protect your capital.
- **Position Sizing:** Determine the size of each trade or investment based on your overall portfolio and risk tolerance. Avoid putting too much of your capital into a single asset or trade.
- **Regular Portfolio Reviews:** Periodically review your portfolio to assess performance and make necessary adjustments. Rebalance your holdings based on changing market conditions and your investment goals.

Psychological Aspects of Investing and Trading

Success in the cryptocurrency market is not just about strategies and analysis; it also involves managing your emotions and maintaining discipline:

- **Avoid FOMO (Fear of Missing Out):** Making impulsive decisions based on hype or fear of missing out can lead to poor investments. Stick to your strategy and make decisions based on analysis, not emotions.
- **Stay Patient and Disciplined:** Whether you're investing for the long term or trading for short-term gains, patience and discipline are key. Avoid overtrading and stick to your plan.

- **Learn from Mistakes:** The cryptocurrency market is a learning experience. Analyze your past trades and investments to understand what worked and what didn't, and use these insights to improve your future strategies.

Case Studies: Successful Investing and Trading
Learning from successful investors and traders can provide valuable insights into effective strategies:

- **Bitcoin Early Adopters:** Investors who recognized Bitcoin's potential early on and held onto their investments through multiple market cycles have seen substantial returns.

- **Ethereum ICO Investors:** Those who participated in Ethereum's Initial Coin Offering (ICO) and held onto their tokens have reaped significant rewards as Ethereum became a leading platform for smart contracts and decentralized applications.

- **Short-Term Trading Success:** Traders who successfully navigated market trends, such as the 2017 bull run or the 2020 DeFi boom, by using technical analysis and disciplined trading strategies have achieved impressive gains.

In conclusion, smart investing and trading in cryptocurrencies require a deep understanding of the market, well-defined strategies, effective risk management, and emotional discipline. By combining these elements, you can navigate the volatile crypto market and maximize your potential for profit. In the next chapter, we will delve into the importance of security in the cryptocurrency space and how to protect your assets from various threats.

Chapter 8: Securing Your Cryptocurrency Investments

As the cryptocurrency market grows, so do the risks associated with storing and managing digital assets. Security is paramount in protecting your investments from hackers, scams, and other threats. This chapter will cover the essentials of securing your cryptocurrency investments, including best practices for wallet management, safeguarding private keys, recognizing scams, and ensuring overall security.

Understanding the Risks

The decentralized nature of cryptocurrencies provides both benefits and challenges. While it offers financial autonomy, it also means that the responsibility of securing your assets lies entirely with you. Key risks include:

- **Hacking:** Cybercriminals target exchanges, wallets, and individual investors to steal cryptocurrencies.

- **Phishing Scams:** Fraudulent schemes designed to trick you into revealing private keys, passwords, or personal information.

- **Malware:** Malicious software that can infect your device and compromise your wallet or private keys.

- **Human Error:** Mistakes such as losing private keys, sending funds to the wrong address, or falling for scams.

Wallet Management

Choosing the right wallet and managing it correctly is crucial for securing your assets. There are several types of wallets, each with different security features:

- **Hardware Wallets:** Physical devices that store your private keys offline, offering the highest level of security. Examples include Ledger Nano S, Ledger Nano X, and Trezor.

- **Software Wallets:** Applications that you install on your computer or mobile device. They are more convenient but can be vulnerable to malware and hacking. Examples include MetaMask, Trust Wallet, and Exodus.

- **Paper Wallets:** Physical documents that contain your private and public keys. They are highly secure if generated and stored correctly but can be lost or damaged.

- **Exchange Wallets:** Wallets provided by cryptocurrency exchanges. They are convenient for trading but are less secure because they are online and managed by the exchange.

Best Practices for Wallet Security:

1. **Use Hardware Wallets:** For long-term storage of significant amounts of cryptocurrency, use hardware wallets to keep your private keys offline.
2. **Secure Software Wallets:** Ensure your software wallet is from a reputable provider and regularly updated to protect against vulnerabilities.
3. **Backup Your Wallet:** Create backups of your wallet and store them in multiple secure locations. For hardware and paper wallets, ensure the backup includes the recovery phrase.
4. **Enable Two-Factor Authentication (2FA):** Add an extra layer of security by enabling 2FA on your wallet and exchange accounts.

Safeguarding Private Keys

Your private keys are the most critical component of your cryptocurrency security. Losing your private keys means losing access to your funds, and exposing them to others means they can steal your assets. Tips for Protecting Private Keys:

- **Never Share Your Private Keys:** Treat your private keys like your bank PINs—never share them with anyone.

- **Store Offline:** Keep your private keys offline, preferably in a hardware wallet or a securely stored paper wallet.

- **Use Strong Passwords:** Protect your wallets and accounts with strong, unique passwords. Avoid using easily guessable information.

- **Be Wary of Phishing Attempts:** Always verify the authenticity of websites, emails, and messages requesting your private keys or personal information.

Recognizing and Avoiding Scams

The cryptocurrency space is rife with scams, from fake ICOs to phishing schemes. Being able to recognize and avoid these scams is essential for protecting your investments.

Common Scams and How to Avoid Them:

- **Phishing:** Fake websites or emails that mimic legitimate services to steal your information. Always double-check URLs and avoid clicking on suspicious links.

- **Ponzi Schemes:** Investment schemes promising high returns with little risk. Be skeptical of guaranteed profits and do your own research.

- **Fake ICOs and Projects:** Scammers create fake projects to raise funds and then disappear. Verify the legitimacy of projects through thorough research and community reviews.
- **Impersonation Scams:** Scammers impersonate celebrities, influencers, or support staff to gain your trust and steal your assets. Always verify identities and communicate through official channels.

Ensuring Overall Security
Beyond protecting your wallets and private keys, there are additional steps you can take to enhance your overall security:

- **Secure Your Devices:** Ensure your devices are protected with up-to-date antivirus software, firewalls, and security patches.
- **Use Encrypted Connections:** When accessing your wallets or making transactions, use a VPN and ensure the website uses HTTPS encryption.
- **Be Discreet:** Avoid publicly disclosing your cryptocurrency holdings. Sharing your investments can make you a target for hackers and scammers.
- **Regularly Monitor Your Accounts:** Keep an eye on your accounts for any suspicious activity and act immediately if you detect any issues.

Case Studies: Security Breaches and Lessons Learned
Examining past security breaches can provide valuable lessons for securing your own investments:

- **Mt. Gox:** Once the largest Bitcoin exchange, Mt. Gox was hacked in 2014, resulting in the loss of 850,000 BTC. This highlighted the risks of keeping large amounts of cryptocurrency on exchanges and the importance of using secure storage solutions.

- **DAO Hack:** In 2016, a vulnerability in the DAO smart contract was exploited, resulting in the theft of $60 million worth of Ether. This emphasized the importance of smart contract security and thorough code audits.

- **Ledger Data Breach:** In 2020, Ledger, a hardware wallet provider, suffered a data breach exposing customer information. While no funds were stolen, the breach underscored the importance of securing personal information and being vigilant against phishing attacks.

Future Trends in Cryptocurrency Security
The cryptocurrency space is continually evolving, and so are the threats and security measures. Future trends in security include:

- **Multi-Signature Wallets:** Wallets that require multiple signatures to authorize transactions, adding an extra layer of security.

- **Decentralized Security Solutions:** Leveraging blockchain technology for decentralized security measures, such as decentralized exchanges (DEXs) and identity verification systems.

- **Improved User Education:** As the industry matures, there will be greater emphasis on educating users about security best practices and the risks associated with cryptocurrency investments.

- **Regulatory Developments:** Increased regulation may lead to more secure and transparent practices within the cryptocurrency space, protecting investors and reducing fraud.

In conclusion, securing your cryptocurrency investments requires a proactive approach and adherence to best practices in wallet management, private key protection, scam recognition, and overall security. By staying informed and vigilant, you can protect your assets from the myriad of threats in the crypto space. In the next chapter, we will explore how to identify and capitalize on emerging trends and opportunities in the cryptocurrency market.

Chapter 9: Navigating Market Volatility: Strategies for Success

Volatility is a defining characteristic of the cryptocurrency market, presenting both opportunities and challenges for investors and traders. While volatility can lead to significant gains, it also carries inherent risks and requires careful navigation. This chapter will explore strategies for managing and profiting from market volatility effectively.

Understanding Market Volatility

Cryptocurrency prices can experience rapid and substantial fluctuations due to various factors, including:

- **Market Sentiment:** Investor sentiment, influenced by news, social media trends, and macroeconomic factors, can drive buying or selling pressure, leading to price volatility.

- **Regulatory Developments:** Regulatory announcements and policy changes can impact market sentiment and trigger price movements.

- **Market Manipulation:** Manipulative trading practices, such as pump-and-dump schemes and coordinated trading activity, can exacerbate volatility.

- **Technological Factors:** Technical issues, software bugs, and network congestion can disrupt trading activity and contribute to price volatility.

Strategies for Managing Market Volatility

While volatility can be unsettling, it also presents opportunities for profit.

Here are some strategies for managing market volatility effectively:

- **Risk Management:** Implement risk management techniques, such as stop-loss orders, position sizing, and portfolio diversification, to protect your investments and minimize losses during periods of high volatility.
- **Long-Term Investing:** Take a long-term perspective and focus on projects with strong fundamentals and growth potential. Avoid making impulsive decisions based on short-term price fluctuations.
- **Dollar-Cost Averaging (DCA):** Use DCA to gradually invest fixed amounts of money at regular intervals, regardless of market conditions. DCA can help mitigate the impact of volatility and reduce the risk of buying at the top of the market.
- **Staying Informed:** Stay updated on industry news, developments, and market trends to anticipate and react to changes in market conditions. Engage with the community and follow reputable sources for reliable information.
- **Technical Analysis:** Use technical analysis tools and indicators to analyze price charts, identify trends, and determine entry and exit points. Technical analysis can help you navigate market volatility and make informed trading decisions.
- **Hedging Strategies:** Consider using hedging strategies, such as options contracts or futures contracts, to protect your portfolio from adverse price movements. Hedging can help offset potential losses during periods of high volatility.
- **Volatility Trading:** Embrace volatility as an opportunity for profit by engaging in volatility trading strategies, such as scalping or momentum trading. These strategies capitalize on short-term price movements and can be profitable in volatile markets.
- **Staying Calm and Disciplined:** Maintain emotional discipline and avoid making impulsive decisions based on fear or greed. Stick to your trading plan and strategy, and don't let emotions dictate your actions during periods of market volatility.

Case Studies: Successful Volatility Management

Examining past examples of successful volatility management can provide valuable insights into effective strategies:

- **Bitcoin's Price Volatility:** Despite experiencing significant volatility throughout its history, Bitcoin has delivered impressive long-term returns for investors who have held onto their investments through market cycles.

- **DeFi Yield Farming:** Yield farming in the DeFi space involves providing liquidity to decentralized exchanges and earning rewards in the form of interest or tokens. While DeFi protocols can be volatile, yield farming strategies have proven profitable for many investors.

- **Options Trading:** Options trading allows investors to hedge their positions or speculate on price movements while limiting their downside risk. Successful options traders use volatility to their advantage and implement strategies to profit from market fluctuations.

Future Outlook and Adaptation
As the cryptocurrency market continues to evolve, volatility is likely to remain a defining feature. To succeed in navigating market volatility, it's essential to remain adaptable and continually refine your strategies:

- **Adaptability:** Stay flexible and adapt your trading and investment strategies to changing market conditions. What works in one market environment may not work in another, so be prepared to adjust your approach accordingly.

- **Continuous Learning:** Stay updated on new trading techniques, risk management strategies, and market developments through research, education, and engagement with the community.

- **Risk Awareness:** Be aware of the risks associated with market volatility and always prioritize the preservation of capital. Never invest more than you can afford to lose, and always conduct thorough research before making investment decisions.

- **Patience and Discipline:** Practice patience and discipline in your trading and investment activities. Avoid succumbing to FOMO (fear of missing out) or panic selling during periods of market volatility, and stick to your long-term goals and objectives.

In conclusion, market volatility is an inherent aspect of the cryptocurrency market that presents both risks and opportunities. By implementing sound risk management practices, staying informed, and remaining adaptable, you can navigate market volatility successfully and capitalize on the opportunities it presents. In the next chapter, we will explore the evolving regulatory landscape of the cryptocurrency market and its implications for investors and traders.

Chapter 10: Navigating Regulatory Challenges in the Cryptocurrency Market

The cryptocurrency market operates in a complex regulatory landscape, with regulations varying significantly across jurisdictions and evolving over time. Regulatory developments can have a profound impact on market sentiment, investor confidence, and the overall trajectory of the cryptocurrency industry. This chapter will explore the evolving regulatory landscape of the cryptocurrency market and its implications for investors and traders.

The Regulatory Environment

Regulatory bodies around the world are increasingly focusing on cryptocurrencies and digital assets, aiming to establish clear guidelines and oversight to mitigate risks and protect investors. Key areas of regulatory focus include:

- **Securities Laws:** Regulators are scrutinizing whether certain cryptocurrencies and token offerings constitute securities and fall under existing securities regulations. This includes initial coin offerings (ICOs), security token offerings (STOs), and tokenized assets.

- **Anti-Money Laundering (AML) and Know Your Customer (KYC) Regulations:** Regulators are imposing AML and KYC requirements on cryptocurrency exchanges and service providers to prevent money laundering, terrorist financing, and other illicit activities.

- **Taxation:** Tax authorities are increasingly addressing the tax implications of cryptocurrency transactions, including capital gains, income tax, and reporting requirements for cryptocurrency holdings.

- Consumer Protection: Regulators are focused on protecting consumers from fraudulent schemes, scams, and misleading information in the cryptocurrency space. This includes warnings about potential risks and educating investors about the speculative nature of cryptocurrencies.

- Stablecoins and Central Bank Digital Currencies (CBDCs): Regulators are paying attention to stablecoins, such as Tether (USDT), and exploring the regulatory implications of CBDCs, issued by central banks.

Impact on Market Sentiment
Regulatory developments can significantly impact market sentiment and investor confidence, leading to price volatility and uncertainty in the cryptocurrency market. Positive regulatory news, such as clarity on regulatory frameworks or favorable legislation, can boost investor confidence and drive market growth. Conversely, negative regulatory developments, such as enforcement actions, bans, or restrictive regulations, can trigger sell-offs and dampen market sentiment.

Testimonials from Listed Coins
Testimonies from Successful NOT Coin and ICE Coin Airdrop Participants

Testimony 1: Maria Sanchez, NOT Coin Airdrop Recipient
"I couldn't believe my luck when I received the NOT Coin airdrop! I had signed up on a whim, thinking it might be a fun experiment. When the tokens hit my wallet, I was skeptical at first. But as the weeks went by, the value of NOT Coin started to climb rapidly. I decided to hold onto them, and within a few months, my initial airdrop had turned into a substantial amount. It was a life-changing experience that gave me the confidence to dive deeper into the world of cryptocurrency."

Testimony 2: James Lee, NOT Coin Airdrop Beneficiary
"Receiving the NOT Coin airdrop was an unexpected surprise that completely changed my financial situation. I had been following the project closely and believed in its potential, so I was thrilled to get in on the ground floor through the airdrop. The value of my NOT Coin holdings grew significantly, allowing me to pay off some debts and invest in other promising cryptocurrencies. This experience showed me the incredible opportunities that crypto airdrops can offer."

Testimony 3: Emma Johnson, ICE Coin Airdrop Participant
"When I got the ICE Coin airdrop, I didn't think much of it. I had participated in a few airdrops before, but none had really amounted to anything significant. This time, it was different. The ICE Coin project gained traction quickly, and the tokens I received increased in value beyond my expectations. I decided to sell a portion to secure some immediate gains and held onto the rest for long-term growth. The ICE Coin airdrop was a fantastic introduction to the potential of strategic crypto investing."

Testimony 4: David Nguyen, ICE Coin Airdrop Success Story
"I was introduced to the ICE Coin airdrop through a friend who was already involved in the cryptocurrency community. I signed up, and a few weeks later, I received my ICE Coins. At first, I didn't pay much attention, but then I saw the project getting more recognition and the price starting to rise. I ended up with a significant profit from what was essentially free money! This experience opened my eyes to the incredible opportunities in the crypto world and motivated me to learn more about investing and trading."

Testimony 5: Olivia Roberts, NOT Coin and ICE Coin Airdrop Enthusiast
"I've participated in several airdrops, but the NOT Coin and ICE Coin airdrops were by far the most rewarding. The value appreciation of these tokens was beyond anything I expected. With NOT Coin, I was able to reinvest my gains into other promising projects, and the ICE Coin airdrop gave me the capital to start my own small business. These experiences have made me a firm believer in the potential of crypto airdrops to provide substantial financial benefits."
These testimonials highlight the transformative potential of cryptocurrency airdrops, showcasing real-world examples of how participants in the NOT Coin and ICE Coin airdrops experienced significant financial gains and newfound opportunities.

Strategies for Investors and Traders
To navigate the regulatory challenges in the cryptocurrency market, investors and traders can consider the following strategies:

- **Stay Informed:** Stay updated on regulatory developments in your jurisdiction and globally. Follow reputable news sources, regulatory announcements, and industry updates to anticipate changes in the regulatory landscape.

- **Compliance:** Ensure compliance with applicable regulations, including AML, KYC, taxation, and reporting requirements. Choose reputable exchanges and service providers that prioritize regulatory compliance and customer protection.

- **Risk Management:** Assess the regulatory risks associated with investing in certain cryptocurrencies or participating in specific activities, such as ICOs or DeFi platforms. Diversify your portfolio and allocate capital prudently to mitigate regulatory risks.

- **Engagement:** Engage with regulators, policymakers, and industry stakeholders to provide input, share insights, and advocate for clear and balanced regulatory frameworks that support innovation while protecting investors and maintaining market integrity.

- **Adaptability:** Stay adaptable and prepared to adjust your investment and trading strategies in response to changing regulatory environments. Monitor regulatory developments closely and be proactive in addressing compliance requirements.

Future Outlook and Evolution
The regulatory landscape of the cryptocurrency market is expected to continue evolving as regulators grapple with emerging technologies and market developments. While regulatory uncertainty may persist in the short term, clearer guidelines and frameworks are likely to emerge over time, providing greater clarity and stability for market participants. By staying informed, adopting a proactive approach to compliance, and navigating regulatory challenges effectively, investors and traders can position themselves for success in the evolving cryptocurrency market.

In conclusion, navigating regulatory challenges in the cryptocurrency market requires vigilance, adaptability, and adherence to compliance standards. By staying informed, engaging with regulators, and implementing sound risk management practices, investors and traders can mitigate regulatory risks and contribute to the long-term growth and sustainability of the cryptocurrency industry.

Vital Questions from The Crypto Millionaire Handbook

What are the fundamental principles of cryptocurrency and blockchain technology that every investor should understand before entering the market?

_____

_____

_____

How can investors identify high-potential altcoins and distinguish them from the myriad of other cryptocurrencies in the market?

_____

_____

_____

What strategies can be employed to maximize profits during a cryptocurrency bull run, and how do they differ from strategies used in bear markets?

_____

_____

_____

How do meme coins differ from other cryptocurrencies, and what unique risks and opportunities do they present for investors?

_____

_____

_____

What role do NFTs (Non-Fungible Tokens) play in the cryptocurrency ecosystem, and how can investors capitalize on the growing NFT market?

_____

_____

_____

What are airdrops in the context of cryptocurrencies, and how can investors effectively participate in and benefit from them?

_____

_____

_____

What are the best practices for securing cryptocurrency investments, including the management of private keys and the use of different types of wallets?

_____

_____

_____

How can investors stay ahead of emerging trends in the cryptocurrency market, such as DeFi, Layer 2 solutions, and interoperability projects?

_____

_____

_____

What are the key regulatory challenges facing the cryptocurrency market, and how can investors navigate these to minimize risks?

_____

_____

_____

How should investors approach risk management in the volatile cryptocurrency market, and what specific techniques can they use to protect their investments?

_____

_____

_____

REFERENCES

Anderson, J. (2022). The Basics of Blockchain and Cryptocurrency. New York: Crypto Publishing House.
- Provides a foundational understanding of blockchain technology and cryptocurrency concepts.

Bennett, L. (2023). Altcoins and the Future of Decentralized Finance. London: TechPress.
- Explores the landscape of altcoins and their role in the DeFi ecosystem.

Carter, M. (2023). Navigating the Cryptocurrency Market: Strategies for Success. San Francisco: Blockchain Insights.
- Offers strategies for investing and trading in the volatile cryptocurrency market.

Davis, R. (2023). The Rise of NFTs: Digital Art and Beyond. Los Angeles: Digital Innovation Press.
- Examines the burgeoning NFT market and its implications for digital ownership.

Evans, P. (2024). Crypto Security: Protecting Your Digital Assets. Chicago: CyberSafe Publications.
- Discusses best practices for securing cryptocurrency investments and managing private keys.

Foster, H. (2022). Regulatory Challenges in Cryptocurrency. Washington, D.C.: Finance & Law Publications.
- Analyzes the regulatory environment surrounding cryptocurrencies and its impact on the market.

Green, A. (2024). Emerging Trends in Cryptocurrency: DeFi, Layer 2, and Beyond. Boston: Innovation Press.
- Identifies and explores emerging trends in the cryptocurrency space, including DeFi and Layer 2 solutions.

Harrison, K. (2023). Airdrops and the Crypto Economy: Opportunities and Risks. Miami: Digital Assets Publishing.
- Provides an in-depth look at the role of airdrops in the cryptocurrency market and how to benefit from them.

Jones, S. (2022). Understanding Market Volatility in Cryptocurrency. Dallas: CryptoDynamics Press.
- Offers insights into managing and profiting from the inherent volatility in the cryptocurrency market.

Smith, L. (2024). Case Studies in Cryptocurrency Success. Seattle: FinTech Publishing.
- Features real-world examples of successful cryptocurrency investments and trading strategies.

THANKS FOR READING. I LOVE YOU ALL. PLEASE DO WELL TO WRITE A REVIEW.